Basic Instruction to Bargello Needlepoint
Detail Guideline to Bargello Needlepoint

DEDICATION

Contents

Basics to Get You Started 1

Tips for Working With Needlepoint Charts and Patterns 10

Basic Threads and Yarns for Needlepoint 16

The Ultimate Guide to Needlepoint Canvas........................ 20

Essential Needlepoint Supplies 25

Bargello Long Stitch Needlepoint Patterns 30

Basics to Get You Started

Needlepoint is worked one stitch at a time on even-weave canvas and is easy to learn. If you are new to needlepoint, here are nine basic things you need to know to get started with your first project.

In just a few hours you will be creating easy needlepoint pieces you'll be proud to display or wear.

01

of 09

What Is Needlepoint? Definition and Brief History Explained

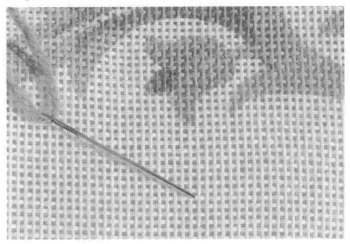

Needlepoint is both creative as well as therapeutic; it engages both the hands as well as the imagination, causing the body to relax and de-stress with the simple gentle rhythm of thread working through the canvas.

Worked in stitch techniques designed specifically for needlepoint, a project can be made with a graph or chart by counting squares and making stitches from them onto canvas; or by filling in a design that has already been painted on the canvas itself.

Needlepoint has been worked for centuries around the world. Learn more about the history of needlepoint and how it differs from other forms of embroidery.

02
of 09
Needlepoint Canvas Facts Every Beginner Should Know

Needlepoint canvas is the ground fabric used to work a project. It comes in a variety of sizes--from very fine canvas that looks like gauze to the traditional coarse crisp fabric. Gain a better understanding of the canvas used to make needlepoint projects in this Ultimate Guide.

Learn about the various types of even-weave needlepoint canvas--from basic to novelty, as well as the perfect size canvas you should use for your first beginner needlepoint project.

03

of 09

Basic Tent Needlepoint Stitches to Get You Started

Tent Stitches are the basic foundation stitches of most needlepoint projects and are also a family of stitches worked diagonally on the canvas. Most diagonal needlepoint stitches are derived from one or all three of the traditional tent stitches.

This easy-to-follow Needlepoint Wiki will show you how to work the three basic tent stitches: Half-Cross, Continental and Basketweave. Included are instructions for right and left-handed beginners as well.

04

of 09

Needlepoint Thread Basics

Not all yarn or thread is suitable for needlepoint, but there are hundreds of fibers that can be used to stitch a needlepoint design. Find out the best yarn and thread types to use in working a beginner needlepoint project.

Learn about textured fibers and novelty needlepoint yarns to use in accenting a specific area of a needlepoint design.

05

of 09

Choosing the Right Needle for Needlepoint

5

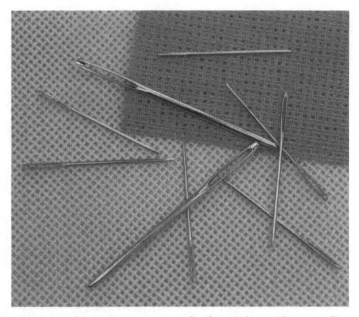

Needlepoint requires a blunt tip tapestry needle for stitching. These needles come in a variety of sizes.

Get tips on the right size needed to work your project as well as different ways to easily and properly thread the needle to make your needlepoint stitches look smooth and even.

06

of 09

Needlepoint Tools and Supplies

Needlepoint requires only a few basic inexpensive tools. Check out these tips for MUST HAVE and WISHLIST items every needle pointer should keep on hand.

Start with the basics like canvas, tapestry needles, yarn and thread; and then as you gain more experience working needlepoint projects, gradually add frames, stretcher bars, and other convenient items to your collection.

07

of 09

Downloading and Printing Free Needlepoint Charts

Here are suggestions as well as a step-by-step tutorial on how to download, enlarge and print needlepoint patterns and charts found online.

You'll learn how to save them to your computer for easy access and to re-use them in other needlepoint projects.

08

of 09

Step-by-Step Instructions for Working a Waste Knot

To begin stitching a needlepoint project requires that you use a waste or away knot. This not sits on top of the canvas to allow the threads to be properly secured on the back.

With these simple instructions, you can learn how to easily make an Away or Waste Knot to get ready for smooth and even stitching.

Continue to 9 of 9 below.

09

of 09

Blocking and Finishing a Needlepoint Project

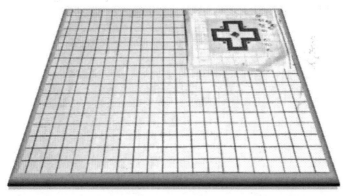

A first needlepoint project, when completed, will most often be slightly warped and a little out of shape. You can easily square up your finished project with a blocking board and a few simple instructions.

Learn how easy it is to do-it-yourself and block your needlepoint to restore the canvas to its original sizing and shape.

Tips for Working With Needlepoint

Charts and Patterns

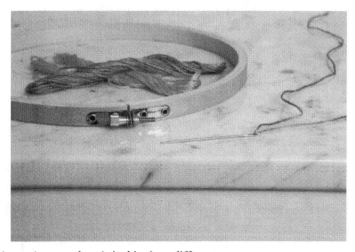

Needlepoint projects can be stitched in three different ways:

Prework: This type of project already has the main design areas worked in basic tent needlepoint stitches. All you need do is stitch the background.

Hand-painted canvas: Needlepoint projects of this type have beautiful hand-painted designs that allow you to stitch creatively using a variety of techniques.

Needlepoint charts: These show the pattern printed on a graph or grid with color squares or symbols. This grid is meant to mimic canvas mesh threads.

Working With a Needlepoint Chart

To work a needlepoint pattern from a chart, each square is counted as one diagonal stitch over the intersection of a vertical and horizontal canvas mesh. If you are familiar with cross stitch and other types of embroidery, working from a needlepoint chart is the same. There is no need to paint a canvas when following a chart.

Using Online Needlepoint Charts

The free needlepoint patterns are charted in color to give you an idea of what the stitched needlepoint designs will look like when completed. However, they may need a little massaging to see them and follow them better. The needlepoint patterns and charts should be downloaded full-size from their links, and then enlarged as needed for printing.

Although charted symbols work well for other types of needlework; they are usually not as effective when reading a needlepoint chart because of the confusion that occurs when attempting to translate symbols into diagonal shaped stitches that are typically used in needlepoint.

The more detailed the needlepoint design, the more colors there will be on the needlepoint chart. Although at first glance, a multi-colored needlepoint chart may look confusing when placed next to a piece of blank needlepoint canvas, you only need to remember these nine tips to understand and be successful in using a chart to stitch needlepoint projects.

Work From the Chart, Not a Traced Design

If the needlepoint chart is not in color, use markers or pencils in the same colors as seen in the completed design photo to make it easier to quickly recognize the shades. This will also help when changing the original colors of a design.

Enlarge the Needlepoint Pattern

The majority of the patterns and charts on this site are sized to fit a standard letter size sheet of paper for ease of printing. This means that the more detailed or larger the finished size of the project, the smaller the squares will be on the page.

For example, a chart for a 14-inch needlepoint pillow front needs to be squeezed down to fit an 8.5 x 11" piece of printer paper. This, however, is not always the optimum working size as the larger the finished pattern, the smaller the squares on the chart, and the harder the pattern will be to follow.

So, if the full-size pattern or chart, when re-sized, is larger than a standard sheet of printer paper, it will print on multiple sheets of paper which can be taped together to create one large pattern.

Always enlarge the entire chart or specific areas of the pattern so that you can closely see the color changes. Make several copies of the needlepoint chart as well—especially if you are working from a needlepoint design book. By making extra copies, you can preserve the original for later use in other needlepoint projects.

Count the Squares, Not the Lines

To make a stitch, remember to count the squares on the chart, not the lines separating them. One colored square on the needlepoint chart represents an intersection of a horizontal and vertical mesh of the needlepoint canvas. Although difficult at first, the grid lines on the needlepoint chart must be ignored when making a stitch. You must focus on the colored blocks instead.

Keep Your Place

To know where you are at all times and to keep your place as you stitch, use a very light-colored highlighter to cross off stitched areas on the printed copy. If you plan to re-use the needlepoint chart, mark off the completed stitches with a pencil. If the needlepoint design is large, use a fine felt-tipped pen to darken every tenth line on the needlepoint chart to make it easier to see where to add stitching accents and to begin background fill areas.

Compare the Chart With the Canvas

Although you are working from a charted pattern with colored squares, when working a needlepoint project, the finished stitching will not be square like the chart because of the

13

basic stitch techniques used. However, compensating stitches, vertical and horizontal straight stitches or surface needlepoint stitch techniques can be used to create the illusion of a square design.

Find the Center of the Chart and Canvas

Unless you know the exact dimensions of the finished needlepoint project, always mark the center of the chart as well as the needlepoint canvas with an insoluble ink pen (never use a ballpoint pen unless it is designated for needlepoint and is completely waterproof); or work basting stitches in light-colored thread on the center horizontal and vertical lines.

Follow the Needlepoint Chart for the First Stitch

In most cases, when using a needlepoint chart, you will begin stitching in the center of the design entire design and canvas; but you can also start with the main design motif. Work outwards in any direction from the center or main motif to complete the needlepoint project.

Making Bargello Needlepoint Stitches

When using a chart for Bargello needlepoint designs or other long stitch needlepoint patterns, remember that each colored square is a thread of the needlepoint canvas; so if one long stitch is made up of four squares, then work over four canvas mesh to complete the entire stitch.

Choose Thread Colors From the Needlepoint Chart

Use the needlepoint chart to help you select thread colors for your project, but keep in mind that the colors may not be exact because of the difference in printer ink or computer screens. If the chart has a color guide in the thread family you have chosen, it will work best in selecting the exact colors used by the needlepoint designer.

Experiment With Other Needlework Charts

Other needlework charts including knitting and cross-stitch can be adapted for working in needlepoint as well. Simply experiment a little and remember to think of the colored charts and symbols as one stitch each to convert the design to needlepoint.

Basic Threads and Yarns for Needlepoint

Needlepoint is worked on even-weave canvas instead of fabric. This canvas is similar to wire mesh that's used in window screens. Both needlepoint canvas and wire mesh are evenly woven; but instead of wire, needlepoint canvas is made with long strong cotton or linen fibers that are 100 percent natural.

Why Is Canvas Used in Needlepoint?

Needlepoint is set apart from all other types of embroidery by the material used to make it. Historically, needlepoint was used for upholstery including furniture and chair covers, pillows, draperies, and rugs.

The even-weave canvas was found to be durable enough to withstand the wear and tear of constant usage, and thus became the material-of-choice for working these types of needlepoint projects.

Over the centuries, as needlepoint developed from being the way to embroider practical home decor items to that of fine art, needlepoint canvas has changed as well to include non-traditional or novelty even-weave materials.

Plastic canvas, perforated paper, and waste canvas are a few examples of novelty materials that are suitable for stitching needlepoint projects.

Sizing and How Needlepoint Canvas Is Made

Needlepoint Canvas is made up of a loosely woven square netting with horizontal and vertical threads that weave over and under each other at evenly spaced intersections. During the manufacturing process, the vertical or warp threads are placed on the weaving loom first and provide the foundation for the canvas. The horizontal or weft threads are then woven back and forth over and under the warp threads to make the final ground fabric used in needlepoint.

Needlepoint stitches are worked at the intersections of the warp and weft threads, covering the canvas entirely when stitching a design.

After the weaving process has been completed, needlepoint canvas is then stiffened with sizing to keep the woven strands in place for stitching a design. This sizing is similar to fabric starch; but made of a stronger solution that when completely dry and polished, will be able to withstand the constant rubbing and pulling of needlepoint yarn as it is worked consistently through the canvas.

A Word About Needlepoint Canvas Quality

Poor quality canvas has scanty sizing, making it limp and easy to tear and pull the canvas strands out of place during stitching. Good quality canvas has sufficient sizing to make it crisp and stiff but is polished enough to make the stitching process smooth and even.

The highest quality needlepoint canvas, made in West Germany, is not only crisp with proper sizing but has a polished look and feel. The more polished the threads, the better the quality of the canvas.

Types of Needlepoint Canvas

There are two basic types of needlepoint canvas—single thread and double thread—including common varieties like Mono, Interlock, and Penelope; as well as novelty examples of even-weave materials that fall in one or both types. Most needlepointers have a type they prefer to use every time they make a needlepoint project.

Every needlepoint project starts with a result in mind. Understanding the basic types of canvas is critical for deciding which kind to use. For example, if your needlepoint project is meant to be a pillow, single thread canvas is most appropriate; if a portrait with detailed areas for the face or hands, then double thread canvas should be used.

How to Use the Ultimate Guide to Needlepoint Canvas

This Needlepoint Canvas Wiki will help you demystify the basics and increase your knowledge. Continue reading to learn what you need to know about your preferred type of needlepoint canvas, and then use your new knowledge to make quality selections when buying canvas for your next needlepoint project.

Every needlepoint project begins with a description of the canvas size needed to work it. This size is called, "Mesh." It is the per-square-inch gauge of the canvas and is represented by the # symbol. For example, #10 canvas has a 10-mesh gauge per inch; #13 has a 13-mesh gauge, and so on for all other sizes of needlepoint canvas, regardless of type.

Calculating Needlepoint Canvas Mesh

There exists a bit of a controversy over how to calculate canvas mesh. Depending on the needlepoint designer, shop owner or instructor, "mesh" or canvas size can be calculated in two different ways—"holes-per-inch" or "strands-per-inch."

Holes-per-inch: Take a look at the #10 canvas sample in the left image above. It shows the number of canvas squares or holes between thread intersections in an inch. This is the size canvas you will get when you ask a typical needlepoint shop owner for a piece of #10 needlepoint canvas.

Strands-per-inch: A small number of needlepoint purists would most likely choose the right image above to calculate canvas mesh. It depicts the number of canvas strands or threads per inch; which closely mirrors the basic definition of "mesh." The problem with this way of calculating mesh is that there is one strand more per inch than holes; and in most cases, needlepoint canvas is not made in odd gauges like #11 (instead of #10 canvas), #15 (instead of #14), #19 (instead of #18) and so forth.

Demystify Canvas Mesh With These Basic Facts

No matter how it is defined, the higher the number of mesh, the finer the canvas. Mesh sizes #18 to #24 are fine enough for delicate and detailed Petit Point projects. As the mesh gets even finer at #32 and #40, the canvas begins to look like transparent gauze fabric.

The lower the canvas mesh size, the larger the squares and holes between the canvas strands. Mesh sizes #3 to #7 have squares large enough to work Quickpoint and needlepoint rugs with heavy Persian or rug yarn.

The Ultimate Guide to Needlepoint Canvas

Needlepoint is worked on even-weave canvas instead of fabric. This canvas is similar to wire mesh that's used in window screens. Both needlepoint canvas and wire mesh are evenly woven; but instead of wire, needlepoint canvas is made with long strong cotton or linen fibers that are 100 percent natural.

Why Is Canvas Used in Needlepoint?

Needlepoint is set apart from all other types of embroidery by the material used to make it. Historically, needlepoint was used for upholstery including furniture and chair covers, pillows, draperies, and rugs.

The even-weave canvas was found to be durable enough to withstand the wear and tear of constant usage, and thus became the material-of-choice for working these types of needlepoint projects.

Over the centuries, as needlepoint developed from being the way to embroider practical home decor items to that of fine art, needlepoint canvas has changed as well to include non-traditional or novelty even-weave materials.

Plastic canvas, perforated paper, and waste canvas are a few examples of novelty materials that are suitable for stitching needlepoint projects.

Sizing and How Needlepoint Canvas Is Made

Needlepoint Canvas is made up of a loosely woven square netting with horizontal and vertical threads that weave over and under each other at evenly spaced intersections. During the manufacturing process, the vertical or warp threads are placed on the weaving loom first and provide the foundation for the canvas. The horizontal or weft threads are then woven back and forth over and under the warp threads to make the final ground fabric used in needlepoint.

Needlepoint stitches are worked at the intersections of the warp and weft threads, covering the canvas entirely when stitching a design.

After the weaving process has been completed, needlepoint canvas is then stiffened with sizing to keep the woven strands in place for stitching a design. This sizing is similar to fabric starch; but made of a stronger solution that when completely dry and polished, will be able to withstand the constant rubbing and pulling of needlepoint yarn as it is worked consistently through the canvas.

A Word About Needlepoint Canvas Quality

Poor quality canvas has scanty sizing, making it limp and easy to tear and pull the canvas strands out of place during stitching. Good quality canvas has sufficient sizing to make it crisp and stiff but is polished enough to make the stitching process smooth and even.

21

The highest quality needlepoint canvas, made in West Germany, is not only crisp with proper sizing but has a polished look and feel. The more polished the threads, the better the quality of the canvas.

Types of Needlepoint Canvas

There are two basic types of needlepoint canvas—single thread and double thread—including common varieties like Mono, Interlock, and Penelope; as well as novelty examples of even-weave materials that fall in one or both types. Most needlepointers have a type they prefer to use every time they make a needlepoint project.

Every needlepoint project starts with a result in mind. Understanding the basic types of canvas is critical for deciding which kind to use. For example, if your needlepoint project is meant to be a pillow, single thread canvas is most appropriate; if a portrait with detailed areas for the face or hands, then double thread canvas should be used.

How to Use the Ultimate Guide to Needlepoint Canvas

This Needlepoint Canvas Wiki will help you demystify the basics and increase your knowledge. Continue reading to learn what you need to know about your preferred type of needlepoint canvas, and then use your new knowledge to make quality selections when buying canvas for your next needlepoint project.

Basic Cheat Sheet on Single Thread Needlepoint Canvas

Double Thread Needlepoint Canvas: Do You Really Need It?

How to Handle Every Needlepoint Canvas Challenge with Ease

What You Probably Don't Know About Canvas Mesh

Every needlepoint project begins with a description of the canvas size needed to work it. This size is called, "Mesh." It is the per-square-inch gauge of the canvas and is represented by the # symbol. For example, #10 canvas has a 10-mesh gauge per inch; #13 has a 13-mesh gauge, and so on for all other sizes of needlepoint canvas, regardless of type.

Calculating Needlepoint Canvas Mesh

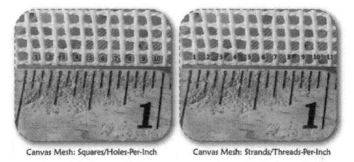

Canvas Mesh: Squares/Holes-Per-Inch   Canvas Mesh: Strands/Threads-Per-Inch

There exists a bit of a controversy over how to calculate canvas mesh. Depending on the needlepoint designer, shop owner or instructor, "mesh" or canvas size can be calculated in two different ways—"holes-per-inch" or "strands-per-inch."

Holes-per-inch: Take a look at the #10 canvas sample in the left image above. It shows the number of canvas squares or holes between thread intersections in an inch. This is the size canvas you will get when you ask a typical needlepoint shop owner for a piece of #10 needlepoint canvas.

Strands-per-inch: A small number of needlepoint purists would most likely choose the right image above to calculate canvas mesh. It depicts the number of canvas strands or threads per inch; which closely mirrors the basic definition of "mesh." The problem with this way of calculating mesh is that there is one strand more per inch than holes; and in most cases, needlepoint canvas is not made in odd gauges like #11 (instead of #10 canvas), #15 (instead of #14), #19 (instead of #18) and so forth.

Demystify Canvas Mesh With These Basic Facts

No matter how it is defined, the higher the number of mesh, the finer the canvas. Mesh sizes #18 to #24 are fine enough for delicate and detailed Petit Point projects. As the mesh gets even finer at #32 and #40, the canvas begins to look like transparent gauze fabric.

The lower the canvas mesh size, the larger the squares and holes between the canvas strands. Mesh sizes #3 to #7 have squares large enough to work Quickpoint and needlepoint rugs with heavy Persian or rug yarn.

Essential Needlepoint Supplies

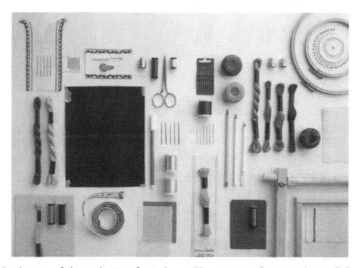

Needlepoint is one of the easiest crafts to learn. To get started, you only need five essential supplies to stitch up your first project. Once you've mastered the basics, you can enhance your stitching experience with eight additional gadgets.

Advanced stitchers who wish to take their needlework to the next level and design their own projects should consider seven more vital tools as well.

5 Basic Needlepoint Supplies You Need to Get Started

Every craft requires basic tools and equipment to start and complete a project. For needlepoint, there are five essentials.

1. Needlepoint Canvas, Pattern, or Chart – Beginners usually start with a design already painted on canvas or a machine-printed one in a needlepoint kit. As you gain experience working on needlepoint projects, you can progress to using patterns or design charts with a blank canvas.

2. Assorted Threads and Fibers – Needlepoint requires specific yarns and fibers. These threads must be strong enough and able to withstand the constant pull and tug as you place stitches on the canvas.

3. Tapestry Needles – Blunt-tipped tapestry needles are necessary for working on needlepoint canvas. They come in several sizes that match the ground fabric you are using for your project, and do not puncture or split the mesh threads as you stitch. Although the needle eye is larger than a typical sewing needle, you can use a needle threader if you need extra help.

4. Embroidery Scissors - To clip threads and cut yarn, you'll need a small pair of sewing scissors with sharp points. Consider buying a pair of nippers or specialty cutters if you like to stitch needlepoint while traveling.

5. Lighting and Magnification - Tiny canvas holes and certain thread colors can be difficult to see in dim light. So make sure to have adequate lighting as well as

magnification when working on your project. A lamp that simulates daylight and a pair of extra-strength reading glasses work best.

8 Needlepoint Gadgets to Enhance Your Stitching

As you become more familiar with needlepoint, you will want tools to make each new project easier to complete. These optional tools will help to take your stitching to new levels:

1. Stretcher Bars or Frames - Experienced stitchers use artist stretcher bars or scroll frames to mount needlepoint canvas and keep their hands free to do surface embroidery, add embellishments, and produce professional-looking results.
2. Masking Tape - Needlepoint canvas edges are rough and require some covering to keep the mesh threads from unraveling. Household masking tape and blue painter's tape are ideal wrappings for protecting these edges.
3. Brass Tacks or Staples - You can attach canvas to stretcher bars with brass thumbtacks, evenly spaced for sufficient tautness. Mount needlepoint on a frame with rustproof staples or hand-stitching.
4. Magnets - Most craft stores sell sets of small painted magnets for needlepoint. You can use them to attach extra needles, scissors, and other tools to the frame or stretcher bars for convenient stitching.

5. Floor or Lap Stands - Perfect for stitching larger needlepoint projects, you can choose from lap or table stands to adjustable floor models that provide the most comfort. Use a clamp or frame weight to fasten a project to a table or counter.

6. Ruler or Measuring Tape - Use at least a 12-inch ruler or a flexible tape measure that has both standard and metric sizes.

7. Waterproof Markers - For help finding the center of a canvas or drawing an outline of a design shape, use permanent waterproof markers. Avoid black or other dark colors as they may show through your completed stitching.

8. Project Bag - After gathering all the supplies you need for a project, you can keep them together in one place. Plastic or cloth bags, wooden boxes, or crates that fit the size of your needlepoint projects are excellent storage solutions.

7 Additional Needlepoint Tools for Advanced Stitchers

Now that you have lots of experience working on a needlepoint project, it's time to expand your skills by creating new designs and making your finished work look as if it was done by a professional:

1. Laying Tool - If a needlepoint project requires stranded thread, then you should use a long stick-like tool or trolley needle to smooth the strands before placing a stitch.

Laying tools are usually made of wood or metal and can be plain or decorative. You can buy them from needlepoint shops or online boutiques.

2. Blocking Board and Pins - For DIY finishing, you will need a blocking board and rustproof push pins to stretch a completed canvas back into shape.

3. Thread Bobbins or Cards - To keep leftover threads from previous needlepoint projects neat and tangle-free, you can store them on bobbins or cards. Group colors or textures together and put each collection away in clear boxes or drawers.

4. Needlepoint Design Books - Browse through needlepoint books to get fresh new design ideas. Visit your local library or used bookstore for the classics to start a personal collection.

5. An Assortment of Acrylic Paints - You can learn to paint on canvas and take your needlepoint to the next skill level. Use water-based acrylic craft paints for filling in shapes or making changes to existing hand-painted designs.

6. Lightbox - This tool works well for tracing patterns from coloring books and similar sources. The lightbox will illuminate the design so that you can make an outline on needlepoint canvas.

7. Needlepoint Pattern Software - With needlework computer software, you can turn photos and clip art images into workable charts—a "Must Have" for creating your personal designs.

Bargello Long Stitch Needlepoint
Patterns

Nothing is more delicate and beautiful than needlepoint worked in the long flowing stitches. The long stitch is one of the easiest techniques to use in working a needlepoint project. Sometimes called the bargello stitch, it is worked straight--either horizontally or vertically on needlepoint canvas, and looks like a smooth satin embroidery stitch when placed in groups side-by-side.

These six needlepoint projects are excellent examples of the quick and easy Long Stitch Technique. Each one can be finished in a weekend--especially if you use #10 or #13 mono or interlock single thread needlepoint canvas.

01

of 06

Hydrangea Blossoms Pattern

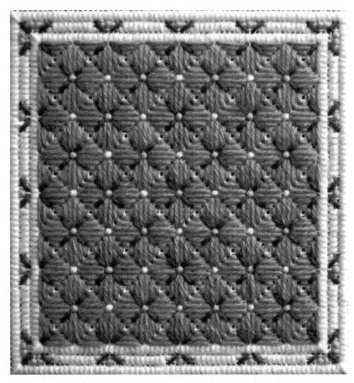

Gardeners, who needlepoint, will thoroughly enjoy stitching this Hydrangea Blossoms Long Stitch Design. You'll work 80 stitches wide as well as high to form a 6.5-inch square finished needlepoint project on #13-mesh mono needlepoint canvas.

For a slightly larger size, use #10-mesh canvas and adjust the thread or yarn thickness to match. Get the needlepoint design and working instructions to complete your version of this simple Bargello needlepoint pattern in a weekend or less.

Turn the finished project into a small pincushion or stuff with potpourri for a fragrant needlepoint sachet.

02

of 06

Rose Romance Design

Talk about fast and easy, this Bargello needlepoint design can be worked in a few hours because of its repeating motif. Once you start, you'll be stitching long stitch roses across the canvas in just a few hours; and in one weekend you can complete an entire needlepoint pillow!

When worked on #18 mono needlepoint canvas, the square design looks lovely finished as an ornament with decorative trim, or made into a top insert for a small keepsake box.

If you're feeling adventurous or are an advanced needlepointer, try working the pattern on Penelope canvas for an interesting effect; or use interlock canvas that works best for Bargello projects. Check out the full design chart and stitch details for the project.

03

of 06

Pumpkin Patch Project

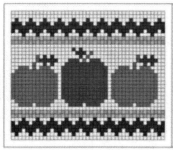 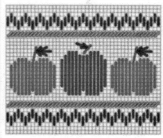

Use this long stitch needlepoint design to work a border or band that can be attached to a tote bag, clothing, pillow or other fashion or home accessory. It is super quick and easy and can be completed in under two hours.

In addition to traditional needlepoint canvas, try stitching the project directly onto a pair of jeans or window curtain tieback with waste canvas. Stitch on perforated paper canvas for greeting and special occasion cards.

You can easily adjust the design to add initials or full name for a personal touch. Instead of the colors used in the charted design, you can choose your favorite ones from the wide range available for most thread types.

Review the pattern instructions for creative ways to stitch and use this long stitch needlepoint pattern.

04

of 06

Ponderosa Pines Pattern

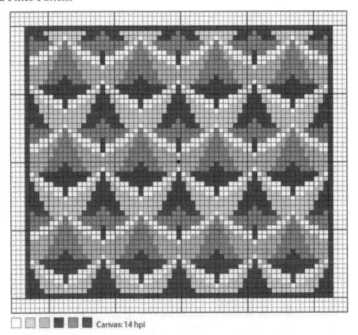

Canvas: 14 hpi

This pattern was inspired by a drive through Spokane, Washington. It features repeating pine trees worked in long stitch. Fast and easy, you'll need dramatic dark monochromatic shades of green to make the pine trees come alive.

Add your choice of brick stitch or Bargello needlepoint border around the entire design once the repeating pine tree motifs have been worked. Choose #13-mesh mono canvas for a finished project that is approximately five inches square.

You can start at the center or at the top to work the project. No matter the starting place, you must pay careful attention to the placement of the first few motifs to avoid counting errors.

05

of 06

Four-Leaf Clover Design

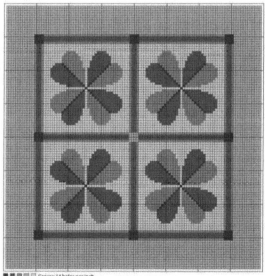

Canvas: 14 holes per inch

The single four-leaf clover in the center of this needlepoint design is worked in long stitch. It can be used to stitch St. Patrick's Day needlepoint gifts, or as a project to learn how to work various textured needlepoint stitches.

A second variation of the design is included with this weekend project. It has four smaller four-leaf clovers that can also be worked in long stitch or basic tent stitches if preferred.

Get the free needlepoint patterns and experiment with your choice of threads and fibers to make the project truly unique.

06
of 06
Bargello Hearts Needlepoint Pattern

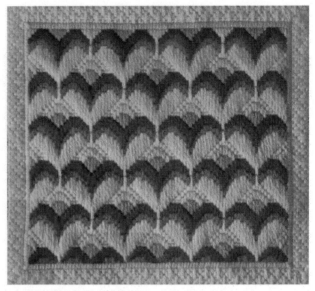

This Bargello Hearts needlepoint pattern may look difficult, but it can easily be worked as a four-way hearts medallion or as a repeating series of simple long stitch hearts for a larger pillow or pin cushion.

Complete with Hungarian Stitch border, both the four-way and straight needlepoint versions are addictive enough to hook you after the first stitch. Be creative as you try the large as well as the small long stitch hearts patterns, adapting them as needed to fit your personal taste.

Basic Instruction to Bargello Needlepoint

Made in the USA
Columbia, SC
06 October 2023

24077743R00026